RED CLOUD'S WAR: AN INSURGENCY CASE STUDY FOR MODERN TIMES

As the Army learned after the invasions of Iraq and Afghanistan, they've done this before. The United States has a history of fighting insurgencies dating back to the mid 19th Century. It is in vogue once again to read historical case studies, particularly those from the 20th Century, to gain insight in how to better prosecute today's insurgent war in Afghanistan. In fact, most of the principles espoused in FM 3-24, the U.S. Army manual on Counterinsurgency, are based on case studies from the 20th Century.[1] But there's at least one very long and similar campaign against a similar insurgent foe: the American Indian Wars. Counterinsurgency today, or "COIN" as it is referred to, is a relatively new American term for counterinsurgency, but the fight with insurgents it refers to is much older-even ancient-when referring to irregular enemies.[2] The U.S. Army Indian Wars of the 19th Century, while being similar, remain little studied in today's COIN academic circles. This paper will specifically be a case study of Red Cloud's War of 1866, which consisted of the various depredations committed by the Sioux, Cheyenne, and Arapahoe upon frontier settlements and emigrants between the years 1863 and 1868.[3] Red Cloud's War remains the only one to have been won by the Indians.[4] While it's true that Custer's defeat at the battle of Little Big Horn was a bigger single battle loss, the Indians ultimately lost the overall war. This study will look at the opening of the Bozeman Trail and how it fundamentally changed the history of Wyoming and Montana. And finally, it will take a detailed look at the Fetterman Massacre at Ft. Phil Kearny, Dakota Territory on December 21st, 1866 and its effects on the Army, government, society and the Indians. Throughout this study, similarities to modern counterinsurgency in Afghanistan will be noted. It shall become clear to the reader that

COIN, although a relatively new term in the American lexicon, is not new in the history of America. This case study will show a lack of proper strategic guidance, failure to properly organize, train and equip the troops, failure to understand a tribally based enemy with a true warrior ethos, reluctance & ignorance in the use of available intelligence, failure to adequately evaluate and use available terrain, and a lack of leadership from the commanding officer.

Many similarities exist between the Indian Wars of the 19th Century and the ongoing COIN efforts in Afghanistan against the Taliban. They include: extremely long lines of supply; rugged terrain, remote forts & outposts, severe winters, tribal based enemy with a warrior culture, and a cunning/mobile/adaptable and elusive enemy whose tactics differ greatly from the U.S. Army.

When finished reading this case study, it will be clear that a little known, but important battle from the Indian Wars had a large effect on the service, the government and U.S. society in general. The relevance of this case study and similar historical military examples may be considered just one more tool in a commander's toolkit when applied to today's ongoing war in Afghanistan. Note that Native American, First Peoples, American Indian are all typically referred to in this paper as "Indian" to: 1) Use the term that was used in 1866, and 2) Be concise.

This document is divided into seven sections: the background and context of the time in America, the U.S. Army and American Indians in 1866; Key Players; the movement of the Army into the Powder River Country; the situation which set the stage for the fight; the Fetterman Massacre; after effects of the battle; and a brief comparison to the Afghanistan Campaign with some lessons learned.

Background

Ten years before the infamous massacre of George Armstrong Custer and his forces at the Little Big Horn, another very similar yet little known battle occurred in the Powder River Country of Wyoming. The Fetterman Massacre as it came to be known was the key and defining battle of Red Cloud's War, and one of the most important of the Indian Wars Campaign. This battle resulted in the largest defeat of U.S. Army troops by American Indians, until eclipsed 10 years later at Custer's Last Stand. In fact, had the Custer debacle not taken place, Fetterman's would probably be a household name. This is a chapter of American History full of high drama, controversy and one that remains shrouded in some mystery. What led to that battle then, is a story of a U.S. War with American Indians over possession and ownership of disputed territory. It was an effort by the U.S. Army to pacify an aroused and dangerous enemy. America, in its Manifest Destiny was expanding west. There was treasure to be had, and to get to it the immigrants had to pass through Indian Country. This is essentially about the strong, newly victorious (in the Civil War) U.S. Government wanting to take something they desired from the American Indians whom they misguidedly perceived as weak. That statement of human nature speaks volumes and is probably true for most of the wars throughout history. Clausewitz said, "War is an act of force to compel our enemy to do our will."[5] In this case, the U.S. Government had a desire to occupy and traverse an area containing the Indian's most sacred hunting grounds. Three traditionally powerful Indian Nations: the Lakota Sioux, Cheyenne, Arapahoe and other allies were determined to resist the momentum of the white man's westward migration. Previous attempts had been made by the government at negotiation, but to no avail. Thus for the Indians, as Clausewitz put it, "War was merely the continuation of policy by other

3

means."[6] This was in essence their most valuable and sacred land, and a very basic survival interest. They were not going to give it up without a fight.[7] This fascinating story is not just about the Fetterman fight; it is also about the Bozeman Trail, Fort Phil Kearny, the defensive minded commanding officer named Carrington, a saber wielding Lieutenant named Grummond and a determined, powerful Sioux leader named Red Cloud.[8] It is important to understand the context of the era, as it is in any historical case study, to see the key role it plays in setting the stage.

The mid 1860's Army was trying to find itself after a long and bloody Civil War. Fiscal constraints and new non-traditional requirements meant that downsizing and reorganization was needed to meet new tasks and challenges. Western posts clearly illustrated the main problem facing the Army in the 1860s: a woefully ineffective logistics system causing a basic lack of resources.[9] On the 21st of December 1866, the U.S. Army and it's perception of the Indian Wars was forever changed by events on the Bozeman Trail. At Ft. Phil Kearny in the Powder River, the Army assigned a very difficult task to a leader and officers who each seemed to be set on their own agenda. Some were vain, overconfident and in search of glory; others were timid, lacking confidence and the leadership skills necessary to do the job.

That day Capt. William J. Fetterman took a force of 81 troops made up of infantry, cavalry and civilians from Ft. Phil Kearny, in an attempt to rescue a wood train which was under attack by the Indians. What followed was the culmination of tensions which had been building for nearly a year, which resulted in utter failure and complete destruction of Fetterman's command. As such, it was the first large scale victory of an

Indian force over a single large U.S. Army command. The events leading up to that day, the massacre and that which followed would help change the Army forever.

The Indian Wars of the 19th Century were the Army's first experience against a true insurgent power. Current Joint doctrine defines an insurgency as an organized movement aimed at the overthrow of a constituted government through the use of subversion and armed conflict.[10] In the case of the Indian Wars, it was a loosely organized, but very long, protracted effort with the desire to weaken the government's will to occupy native lands.[11] Thus counterinsurgency (COIN) as it applies in this case would include the application of DIME power across the full spectrum of the U.S. government. Of course, none of this was known in the mid 1800's. The U.S. government viewed the situation against the plains Indians as an uprising which would be quickly defeated. By today's standards, most events of 1866 in the Powder River Campaign are examples of how not to prosecute COIN.

In the first decade of the new millennium, events have shown that the successful prosecution of COIN campaigns will be a key skill required of the U.S. Army. In its Operating Concept 2016-2028, the Army has stated that for the foreseeable future, as part of "full spectrum operations" they will continue to focus on capabilities to conduct effective and sustained counterinsurgency operations.[12] "Learn and adapt" has become the modern COIN imperative for U.S. forces.[13] Unfortunately, through its history the Army has had to relearn the principles of COIN on the go while conducting operations against adaptive insurgent enemies. Accordingly, it is emphasized repeatedly throughout the Army's FM 3-4, Counterinsurgency. It follows that by studying a key part of a classic COIN campaign like Red Cloud's War is important for today's leaders. They can then meld these lessons learned with others, and then apply them on tomorrow's battlefield.

Up until the early 1860's, relations between American Immigrants and Native Americans were relatively peaceful. The primary route west in the mid-19th Century was the Oregon Trail, and the peace enabled by the Treaty of Fort Laramie in 1851 allowed its use. That treaty between the U.S. government and the various tribes of the plains and Rocky Mountain regions was a key enabler allowing the passage of settlers, building of roads and stationing of troops along the Oregon Trail. But the United States did not always abide by the terms of the treaties it made with the Indians. An example of a broken treaty comes from the summer of 1865, and the Powder River Expedition commanded by General Patrick Connor. He led that expedition into the Powder River Country and gave strict and unequivocal orders, "You will not receive overtures of peace or submission from Indians, but will attack and kill every male Indian over twelve years of age."[14] After prosecuting the campaign for some time with dubious results, Connor prepared to take to the field again in early autumn but it wasn't meant to be. The western military districts had been recently reorganized, and Connor's harsh orders gave his superiors at headquarters visions of another Chivington massacre. In effort to prevent another tragedy, Gen Pope stated, "If any such orders as Connor has given are carried out, it will be disgraceful to the government and cost him his commission if not worse!"[15] Connor's expedition did much to inflame tensions in the Powder River Country in 1865.

The drawdown of the post Civil War Army and white migration west were seminal events of the mid 19th Century. Previously, the Pikes Peak gold rush of 1859 brought large numbers of settlers travelling through the plains to the front range of the Rocky Mountains. In doing so, they disturbed buffalo migration patterns, violated traditional Indian hunting grounds, and killed large numbers of animals both for food and sport. The migration required long supply lines to support the new frontier. Those long supply lines moving through the plains provided ample opportunity for conflict. By the mid 1860's, many of the immigrants passing along the various trails chose a shortcut through the Powder River Country on their way to the gold fields.

Following the Civil War, the Army reorganized via the Act of July 28, 1866 to better perform what were its two main efforts: the Wars against the American Indians in the west, and the supervision and security in the post Civil War Reconstruction of the South. The Western Theater fell into two divisions: The Division of the Missouri and the Division of the Pacific, with separation occurring along the Continental Divide.[16] They further subdivided into departments due to their sheer size: the Departments of the Missouri, Dakota and Platte. The Department of the Platte contained the Powder River Country, and was commanded by Major General Phillip St. George Cooke from its headquarters in Omaha. The Act of 1866 laid the foundation for the postwar Regular Army, and the forces assembled under this law fought the plains wars of 1866-69.[17] Note that in the 1866 regular Army most of the grades from lieutenant to general were filled with comparatively youthful veterans of the war, nearly all with brevetted rank.[18] The Powder River country was the traditional land of the Crow nation. It was a land rich in verdant natural resources. Buffalo, deer & bear, as well as many other forms of game were abundant. The rivers teemed with fish, and the land in general was well watered from the runoff of the Bighorn Mountains. It had everything needed for the

Indian's sustainment and survival. Obviously a land this advantageous to movement and settlement was also very attractive to immigrants. If nothing else, it was easy passage to the goldfields of Montana.[19]

White westward movement had eventually pushed the Lakota Sioux, Cheyenne & Arapahoe into Powder River basin. The resultant conflict and war with the Crow Nation caused great bloodshed and loss of the territory by the Crows. The sacred hunting grounds were now in possession of the three victorious tribes. The Sioux had originally come from the Great Lakes region. All these tribes were master horseman, and over time became skilled and fearsome mounted warriors. It is important to note how much different their tactics were in comparison with the U.S. Army of the time. Indians fought as individuals: their tendency was for no formal organization and lacked a unified plan of attack. Instead, an Indian war party operated as "a body of loosely organized individuals acting toward a common cause." Normally they attacked as raiding parties using guerilla tactics aimed at stealing horses, cattle or a quick kill and scalping.[20] These masterful mounted warriors viewed the land along the Bozeman Trail as important not only from a hunting, sustainment and living space perspective, but regarded much of the land as "sacred ground" to be defended to the death. The Powder River Country from the Big Horn Mountains to the Black Hills loomed large in Indian oral history and myths. It was central to the culture of the Plains Indian tribes. Also engrained in their history and philosophy was the warrior ethos.[21] The Plains Indians rarely made war in the white man's sense, but instead raided in a guerilla fashion. Their type of warfare was with other tribes over land boundaries. Thus mass migration of white settlers to the plains amounted-in their eyes-to a new tribe

8

trespassing the arena of an ancient war.[22] While they've been called the finest light

cavalry in the world, they seemingly had more limitations than capabilities.[23] Their

endurance was unequaled and they were skilled bowmen, and they knew how to use

terrain to their advantage[24] For the Army, these guerilla skills and tactics preferred a

ratio of ten to one (soldiers to Indians) when fighting an Indian Campaign. This was a

ratio consistent with the guerilla campaigns of the twentieth century.[25]

The irregular mission of the western Army in 1866 had some special conditions

which set it apart from more orthodox military assignments (similar to today in

Afghanistan). Certain basic counterinsurgency elements were clearly present:

movement leaders, combatants, their own political cadre, and a mass base.[26] Here

similarities may be drawn between the Indian Wars and Afghanistan. First, it faced an

enemy that blended extremely well with the non combatants. Indians could switch

rapidly from friend to foe, making it difficult to distinguish one from the other. Second,

Indian service placed the U.S. Army soldiers in opposition to a people that could arouse

conflicting emotions. Militarily, the attitude of the troopers was ambivalent: along with

fear, distrust and loathing, there was curiosity, admiration, sympathy and even

friendship. Third, the Indian mission gave the army a foe that fought unconventionally in

techniques, tactics and aims of warfare.[27] These special conditions made the army

seem to function not so much as a military, but as a police force performing "wide area

security" (as its known today). It tried to perform this unconventional mission with very

conventional organization, methods and means. The result was an Indian record that

contained more failures than successes. Military leaders failed to develop a formal doctrine of Indian relations primarily because in their mind it was a temporary situation that would be pacified quickly. In reality it lasted nearly 100 years.

This was very similar to the thinking early on in both the Iraq and Afghanistan Wars. If there was an Indian Wars strategy, it could be summed up as explained by the Board of Indian Commissioners to Red Cloud in 1871, was for "the Great Father to put war-houses all through Indian Country."[28] As later observed by General Edward Ord while commanding the Department of the Platte, "building posts in their country....demoralizes them more than anything except money and whiskey."[29] Both Generals Sherman and Sheridan favored this approach as well. However, it failed mainly due to the small size of the army.

The United States Army had contracted from 2.1 million men at the end of the Civil War, to approximately 13,000 in 1866. It just was not large enough to garrison the posts everywhere they were needed, let alone to man the larger ones located in areas of higher concern. By contrast the Indians were masters at guerrilla warfare. Some Army officers even spoke of adopting those same techniques for use against them. But it never got beyond the discussion phase, and there was no formal strategy training program developed for fighting Indians.[30] The bottom line was that the settlers demanded protection in visible close proximity, and the army would have to provide it.[31]

The desire for gold and the wealth resulting from it was a strong motivation in the mid 19th Century. The first serious cause of migration west was the California Gold Rush of 1849 primarily using the Oregon Trail. This was followed by the Colorado Pikes Peak rush of 1859, and then the Montana Gold Rush of 1862-63. The latter eventually led to the discovery and opening of Bozeman Trail. With the existence of the already well established Oregon Trail, what generated the need for the Bozeman Trail? Gold was discovered in 1863 in the vicinity of Bannack, Virginia City and prieviously in Helena, Montana Territory. Settlers and miners desired a shorter more economical routed to the Montana goldfields. The Oregon Trail required travel West to Salt Lake City, then North a few hundred miles to the goldfields. John Bozeman, pioneer Montana settler discovered a much shorter route thru the Powder River Country. Instead of going west from Ft Laramie to Salt Lake City, it veered northwest across what is now Wyoming along the Big Horn Mountains to the Yellowstone River, finally turning to the west over what was to become Bozeman Pass. While being significantly shorter, this new trail had one major difficulty: it passed through the sacred Indian hunting grounds of the Powder River. An alternate route had been scouted by the famous western mountain man Jim Bridger running west along the Big Horn mountains thus avoiding the contested territory. But it lacked the resources in such abundance on the eastern side.

If it had only been a few wagons passing through periodically, it probably wouldn't have been any more hazardous than any other western trail. But this was not just a wagon train now and then. In the short period from 1864-1866, more than 3500 civilians used the Bozeman Trail to find a new life in the Montana Territory.[32] In 1866 alone, roughly 2000 civilians traversed the trail in over 1200 wagons nearly doubling the previous two years.[33] The Indians watched this "invasion" with ever increasing resentment. In the summer of 1866 it boiled over into open warfare with the United States.

Another reason for the large mid 19th Century westward migration was the large numbers of demobilized Civil War soldiers now without work. They saw the west as the chance for a new beginning with boundless opportunities. That combined with the Homestead Act and the building of transcontinental railroad brought large numbers of settlers into direct conflict with the Indians. The Homestead Act of 1862 was a significant milestone, as it allowed any American citizen-for the cost of $14 to acquire 160 acres of land. After working and living on the land for 5 years, they paid an additional $7 which then gave them legal title and deed to the property. That works out to about 13c an acre, clearly a major incentive for many. This really got the wagons moving westward.

Up until this point, there were only a few choices for travelling west: Conestoga wagon, stagecoach, horse or feet. With the opening of new lands, the resultant gold rushes and desire of the government to replenish treasure spent on the Civil War, all combined to generate the need for safer transportation. This Congress authorized construction of the transcontinental railroad in the Pacific Railroad Act signed by President Lincoln in 1862. The tracks were to be laid parallel to the already well established Oregon Trail. As construction progressed, even more white migration followed the rails; demobilized Civil War veterans, immigrants and speculators, all populating the new towns that sprang up along the tracks taking advantage of cheap land. An unfortunate result of railroad construction was that it went directly through the north/south migrating buffalo herds. Mass killing by white commercial hunters had become common. This killing was rarely for food, but more often for the lucrative buffalo skin trade (or for sport). These factors all combined to further anger the Indians and make them more susceptible to rhetoric from their radical elements who wanted war. Again, this proved to be a significant threat to their survival interests.

Was an insurgency occurring in the Powder River Country of U.S. Dakota Territory? One could argue the Indians felt that way. They viewed the Bozeman Trail as a white invasion into their sacred hunting grounds. That was unacceptable particularly for the Lakota Sioux and Cheyenne tribes who had been continually pressured west by white migration. This incursion into the last bastion of Sioux and Arapahoe dominance, forced the Indians even further west until they were pressed up against the Big Horn Mountains. This was another threat to their survival interests. This land had been officially ceded to them by the Harney-Sanborne Treaty of 1865.[34] Sioux leaders Red Cloud and Man Afraid of His Horses made clear their opposition to white movement or any Army permanent presence along the Bozeman Trail, at the Ft. Laramie Peace Commission of 1866. After listening to white overtures and other tribes subsequent acquiesce, and hearing about the Army plans to garrison three forts along the trail, the Lakota leaders remained steadfastly unwilling to compromise. Just prior to their hasty departure in anger, Red Cloud was quoted saying, "The Great Father sends us presents and wants us to sell him the road, but white chief goes with soldiers to steal road before Indians say yes or no!"[35] At that point they stormed out of the council, gathered their people and swiftly departed to the North-vowing to attack any whites who travelled this route. Few could dispute the logic of their argument. Thus clearly the growing number of settlers passing through the Powder River Country on their way to Montana, and the proposed U.S. Army presence for their protection, provided the match to ignite a conflagration of open warfare.

Key Players

Col Henry B. Carrington. One of the central characters in this drama, Carrington was selected to commanded the Mountain District of the Department of the Platte headquartered at the yet to be established Ft. Phil Kearny. A Yale graduate from Ohio, Henry Carrington had at times been a teacher, engineer, scientist & lawyer. Working as Ohio Adjutant General prior to the Civil War, in 1861 he was politically appointed to a position in the 18th infantry.[36] Carrington spent most of the Civil War as recruiter where his maneuvering generally occurred in political circles. As such he was generally well regarded by his seniors, but not by subordinates because of his lack of actual command and combat experience. He had nevertheless acquired a methodical habit of leadership and led mostly through the written order. His political connections probably helped him gain the post war command of the18th Infantry and the Mountain District. His lack of combat and command experience became a lightning rod within his men as they were thrust into hostile Indian Country in 1866.[37]

Capt William J. Fetterman. Another of the central characters, William J. Fetterman possessed a sterling record of combat in the Civil War and was considered a genuine war hero. His battle honors include the battle of Stones River in Tennessee, and Sherman's Georgia Campaign. His reputation for bravery came with an aggressive and confident attitude which became contagious to those under his command, a useful attribute in combat. The tendencies he had displayed in battle during the Civil War were very much indicative of things to come. Fetterman was promoted to brevet Lieutenant Colonel in the Civil War, then retained but downgraded (as were nearly all officers) to captain in post-war Army.[38] A very competent and well regarded officer, he had no training or understanding of Indian fighting tactics, but instead believed that traditional

Army military strategy would carry him to victory as it had in the past. Young Captain William J. Fetterman brought his offensive mindset developed in Civil War success with him to Ft Phil Kearny in the fall of 1866.

Chief Red Cloud. The last of the central characters is Chief Red Cloud of the Lakota Sioux. An imposing figure, Red Cloud was the bravest of brave and a key leader of his tribe. He had gained a reputation amongst the Lakota as "a man with whom to be reckoned."[39] There is story of Red Cloud rescuing a Ute warrior who had fallen from his horse into a river. After dragging him to shore, he promptly killed and scalped the enemy Ute.[40] It is a testimony to his great warrior prowess that his scalp shirt, now housed in the Buffalo Bill Historical Center in Cody, Wyoming, allegedly contains some eighty scalps.[41] His people had come to the conclusion that they could not tolerate the threat to survival which the whites and especially the soldiers presented by invading and occupying his Powder River Country. By midsummer 1866, Red Cloud felt that the Indians now possessed a force strong enough to defeat them in battle and force the Army to withdraw. He relentlessly pursued this end, and would listen to no one who suggested another scenario (either the U.S. government or Indian agents). At the Ft Laramie Peace Commission of 1866, his actions made it clear that he would sign no treaty and would fight to prevent the establishment of forts and soldiers in his country, or travel along the Bozeman Trail. Chief Red Cloud is credited as the mastermind behind both the siege of Ft Kearny and Fetterman Massacre. Within the insurgency coalition, Red Cloud shared overall Indian coalition leadership with another chief, Young Man Afraid of His Horses.[42] An unusually adept leader, it is generally accepted that Red Cloud's way was to use his brain in planning, and then use his iron will ensuring their execution.[43]

The Army takes the Trail

Ft. Laramie was the "center of important interests to the people of the West" in June 1866.[44] The Ft. Laramie Peace Commission was an effort by U.S. government and the Indian Commission to gain Indian approval for movement along the Bozeman Trail, and for the U.S. Army garrisons there to protect the Immigrants. If this Peace Commission had been successful in getting the approval from all the tribes involved, there is little doubt that later tragedies would have been avoided. Instead, Margaret Carrington said that the failure of the treaty and Red Cloud's departure in anger held, "ominous portents for the future."[45] She was referring to the extremely difficult tasks of building new forts, securing the trail and ensuring safe movement with a command that was "barely sufficient to do its expected work on the basis of permanent and reliable peace," let alone in hostile Indian Country.[46]

On June 17, 1866 Carrington's long column departed Ft. Laramie with the eight companies of the 2nd Battalion of the 18th Infantry and its 226 wagon train, taking possession of the trail with the first destination being Ft. Reno.[47] What's important here is not the obvious spectacle of such a large train hitting the trail in all its pomp and glory, but what was missing. Why the force was predominately infantry instead of cavalry is unknown. Against this mobile enemy, General Sherman himself remained convinced that, "cavalry is the most efficient arm of the service for existing conditions in Indian Country."[48] While at Ft. Laramie, Carrington had made repeated requests of the post commander for his promised 100,000 rounds ammunition, horses and wagon drivers. But the requests fell on deaf ears, and were never to be had. The fact is that he

16

departed with just a fraction of what had been promised, and what they needed to properly perform the task they were ordered to. This would be a reoccurring problem for Carrington and his men in the Powder River Campaign.[49]

Upon arrival at Fort Reno on June 28, it was immediately clear this was an austere and remote post nestled on a plateau above the windswept valley of the Powder River. The location had few redeeming qualities, beyond that it was conveniently halfway to the planned location of Ft Kearny, and had abundant supplies of timber and semi alkaline water immediately available. It was clear that Ft. Reno had essentially become an open post in disrepair, and immediate efforts were made to repair the stockade.[50] Carrington relieved two companies of the 5th U.S. Volunteers who manned the garrison since the Civil War. Those troops were mustered out and immediately replaced by one of Carrington's 2nd Battalion companies.[51] Also present at the post was a company of Winnebago Indian Scouts, and they expressed their desire to stay and continue service. Strangely, Carrington turned them down because he felt having present sworn enemies of the Sioux would only serve to further antagonize the already hostile Indians.[52] In retrospect, the benefits in keeping such a valuable intelligence and Indian fighting resource far outweighed the possible disadvantages.

In preparation for any COIN operation, one of the key tasks is intelligence preparation of the battlefield. This includes defining the operational environment, evaluating the threat and determining threat Courses of Action (COA).[53] The question then, is whether Col Carrington did anything like intelligence preparation of the battlefield. This was a golden opportunity to take advantage of a good intelligence source. But it turned out to be an opportunity lost. The use of Indians against Indians was not a new concept, and had been employed repeatedly with much success throughout the Indian Wars (and subsequently in other counterinsurgencies), and many commanders testified emphatically as to their worth.[54] These Indians would have been invaluable not only as scouts, guides and trailers, but could have been used to plus up his troop strength as well-something Carrington sorely needed. The Army Reorganization Act of 1866 authorized up to 1,000 Indian scouts.[55] One could argue that had Carrington taken advantage of this offer, for a number of reasons the Fetterman Massacre may have never happened. Their job complete at Ft. Reno, the military train and forces departed on July 9th for Ft. Phil Kearny, with Indians ominously observing them every step of the way.

By mid July 1866 Carrington and his force arrived at the location he had chosen for the fort. His first task was to build the post, and accordingly he adopted a defensive posture for construction of the fort. His primary reason was that those were his orders. In his eyes he was further justified by the shortage of troops, ammunition and equipment.

By concentrating on building and establishing the fort at the expense of offensive operations, he was following orders and doing exactly what he was sent there to do. This played to Carrington's strengths, for with little to no experience in training or commanding troops for battle; he was well schooled in engineering and design, perfect for the tasks at hand.[56] In his view, he was sent to the Powder River Country to repair one and build two other forts along the Bozeman Trail, and in doing so establish the Mountain District of the Platte, and that's exactly what he would do. His defensive mindset is further reflected in a letter sent to his boss Brig Gen Phillip Crooke (Head of

Dept of Platte HQ at Omaha), in which he stated, "My ammunition has not arrived; neither has my Leavenworth supply train-I am equal to any attack they may make, but have to build quarters and prepare for winter, escort trains, and guaranty(sic) the whole road first."[57]

The site Carrington selected for the fort was located on a natural plateau between the Big and Little Piney Creeks. It was to be constructed similar to a classic western stockade type fort. Resembling a parallelogram, it was nominally 600 by 800 feet in dimensions making it one of the largest forts ever built in the frontier west. As a student of military engineering, Carrington prided himself in the fort's design. The post was enclosed by formidable stockade of heavy pine logs eight feet high (which had to be hauled from the Pinery in the Bighorn mountains roughly five miles away), enfilading blockhouses in the diagonal corners with portholes for cannon, firing notches every fifth log, gates on every side and five guard stands which allowed for full surveillance 24 hours a day both inside and out.[58] One of the first tasks was to erect the flagpole, and the troops stated that, "the flagpole, an awesome sight: the first garrison to fly the U.S. flag between the North Platte and the Yellowstone Rivers."[59] Later upon inspection after construction was completed, General W.B. Hazen stated that the post was, "the best he had ever seen, except for one built by the Hudson's Bay Company in British America (Ft. Vancouver)."[60]

Carrington's stated reasons for locating the fort where he had were threefold: first that it occupied the very heart of the Indian hunting grounds; second that it was a natural "neutral ground" between the tribes and was a favorite field to all; and last that is was a natural crossroads for movement, hunting and supply for the Indians.[61] In a nutshell, he had placed the location deep in the heart of Indian Country literally guaranteeing heavy contact. On July 16th shortly after construction was started, the Indians sent an emissary to the post warning them of trouble if they did not leave.[62] Also on the 16th of July, the first two of Carrington's men (civilians) were killed during an Indian raid. The next day the 1st Army troops were killed. The following is a concise list of attacks that occurred by date:

- 17 July: 2 troops killed, 3 wounded; 6 civilians in Gazzon party killed

- 22 July: 1 civilian killed, one wounded; 7 mules lost

- 23 July: 3 civilians killed, one train destroyed

- 24 July: 1 troop killed

- 29 July: 9 civilians killed, 1 wounded

- 14 August: 2 civilians killed

- 17 August: 24 animals stolen

- 8 Sept: 20 mules stolen within 1 mile post

- 10 Sept: 33 horses and 78 animals stolen, hay mowing machines destroyed

- 14 Sept: 1 troop killed

- 16 Sept: 1 troop missing and presumed killed

- 17 Sept: 48 cattle stolen

- 23 Sept: 3 civilians killed

- 27 Sept: 1 troop killed, 2 civilians killed[63]

There were clear and menacing indications that the Indians intended to force the troops out of their sacred land. Margaret Carrington summarized life that summer and early fall by saying, "alarms were constant; attacks upon trains were frequent, and this kind of visitation continued during the whole season."[64] The Indians were becoming more emboldened with every successful raid. This pattern gave clear indications of increasing hostilities, and should have warned Carrington that something big was on the horizon.

On August 3, Capt Nathaniel C. Kinney took two companies of infantry and proceeded 90 miles north to the Big Horn River to build and garrison the 3rd post on the Bozeman Trail.[65] On August 12th they established Fort C.F. Smith. This post was much smaller than Fort Kearny, consisting of a 125 foot square stockade and made of adobe (mud) bricks and wood for protection, with bastions for concentrated defense. At its most robust in 1867, tiny Fort C.F. Smith would boast a garrison of nearly 400 troops.

Recipe for Disaster

The terrain in which the forts were located left much to be desired. Fort Phil Kearney was built on a plateau between the two forks of the Little Piney Creek. It was surrounded in all quadrants by higher terrain and dominated by Lodge Trail Ridge to the northeast. This made it very easy for the enemy to watch the soldier's every movement, and for them made the gathering of intelligence a simple task. This intelligence gathering was important, as Indian scouts observed the soldiers developing tendencies, which were later used in planning future attacks. Another major disadvantage of the location was the lack of available nearby timber and hay sources. That resulted in a daily trek of approximately five miles through very hostile territory by the wood and hay trains, and required risking the troops in non-combat oriented tasks outside the stockade. This opportunity was too inviting for the hostiles, and running this daily gauntlet of death resulted in many casualties. On the other hand, one terrain advantage for the Army was the location of Pilot Hill just south of post. It was here that Carrington

21

did a very smart thing: he located a signal station there which he used for early warning, to communicate with outlying lumber and hay mowing detachments, and to watch the approaches of the Bozeman Trail. While it didn't mitigate being surrounded by higher terrain, it was the best part of a bad situation.

Carrington justified the location in his official report as "guaranteeing contact," and at that he was very successful.[66] However, the site of the fort had drawbacks including: it was the most remote U.S. Army post; it was far from the closest signal station allowing communications with headquarters, the supply line was as long as you could get in 1866, it was surrounded by high terrain deep in hostile territory, and there were no closely available subsistence resources. The bottom line is that Carrington was stuck between a rock and a hard place: he had to find a location that balanced the need for defense, water; wood and proximity to the Bozeman Trail yet ensure contact with the enemy. The 2nd Battalion of the 18th Infantry had come to the Powder River country equipped primarily for one task: building the posts and establishing the Mountain District of the Department of the Platte. Once there, they found another more important problem thrust in their lap: open warfare against an insurgent force. The battalion had been equipped with the men, arms, and supplies to build and garrison forts, not to wage war with an active enemy.[67] But there was another larger issue: not only were they undermanned but the makeup of troops and their weapons left much to be desired. Carrington's force was destined to wage war on a swift horsebound foe. That job required a mounted force, most likely a combination of cavalry and infantry. While the bulk of this garrison was made up of mounted infantry, they were short of the required mounts. This meant that most patrols would be on foot. Additionally, the troops were not equipped with the right weapons for the type of warfare they faced. They were outfitted with old muzzle loading Springfield rifles from the Civil War, rather than newer Spencer carbines and breech loading rifles. The civil war era muskets had to be loaded from the muzzle with powder and ball in a paper cartridge, and a percussion cap for ignition. Breech loading weapons used ammunition which combined ignition, propellant and projectile within a single metal cartridge. The breech loaded metal cartridge allowed faster rate of fire, greater velocity and accuracy.[68]

As we shall see, this fact did not go unnoticed by the Indians and was one of the reasons for the tactics they developed. Improper arms should be considered a key factor in the outcome: muzzle loading Springfield rifles had a direct negative effect on outcome of the Fetterman Battle; later acquisition of breech loading "trapdoor" Springfield rifles and their use in both the Wagon Box and Hayfields fights of 1867 was a key factor in their success. One could reasonably argue that if the force Carrington sent to rescue the wood train on December 21st had been cavalry and *mounted* infantry and were equipped with seven shot Spencer repeating rifles, the outcome might have been significantly different. Therefore we see that these factors influenced the outcome of the December 21st battle: not enough horses, incorrect weapons, and finally not enough troops to do the job. Clearly, sending only one battalion comprised of seven infantry companies and one cavalry company to man three separate forts, offensively patrol and protect work detachments and trains along the trail, was not enough to do those tasks. Available intelligence provided by both native sources as well as civilian guides like Jim Bridger showed the troops were clearly outnumbered. There were indications that the hostiles had villages numbering in the 1000's of lodges preparing to wage war against a couple hundred U.S. troops. Carrington was not blind to this information and knew that he was woefully undermanned, and had submitted repeated requests for additional troops. In his official report dated January 3rd, 1867, he refers to the disaster and says "it vindicates my application that if I had received those (troops) assured to me by both telegram and letter, I could have kept up communications and opened a safe route for emigrants next spring."[69] To summarize then, the demise of Fetterman's command resulted from: improper choice of terrain, lack of supplies, incorrect weapons, the wrong type and number of troops, and allowing the enemy to dictate the time/place of the battle.

The Situation Fall 1866

In the fall of 1866, the situation was worsening by the day. The garrison was involved in an insurgent war but didn't know it. Did the nation know? One common feature of insurgencies is that the target government generally takes a while to recognize that an insurgency is occurring.[70] Western newspapers of the time proclaimed a "full scale war" in the Powder River Country; but in official circles the spirit of Indian Superintendent Taylor's "most cordial feeling" continued to prevail.[71] Locally, the enemy was watching every move the troops made, gathering intelligence, and making almost daily attacks. Indications were that serious trouble was on the horizon.

The tactics of the Lakota Sioux had been very successful in harassing communications and supplies moving along the Bozeman Trail. Despite that fact, supplies continued to reach the forts. On the 17th of September, a large supply train reach Ft. Kearny bringing 60,000 rounds of much needed ammunition as well as grain for the horses.[72] Feed grain was an important supply item, since Army horses were larger and they relied almost solely on feed rather than native grass for sustenance.

24

Conversely, the smaller, faster Indian ponies who subsisted solely on native grass had a distinct advantage in a supply limited situation. Nonetheless, the around the clock raids continued, and were growing larger as the Indians confidence grew. The losses on livestock and to a lesser degree people, continued to mount. Little by little troopers and civilians working the lumber and hay trains, and camping at the outlying detachments were being picked off. The Indians were constantly modifying their tactics as they analyzed how the troopers reacted to each skirmish.

This is very similar to the situation in Afghanistan against the Taliban. Over the years, they have proven very adept at modifying their tactics as the Army adjusts to them. The Indian Wars soldiers were not equally adept at recognizing changes and modifying their tactics in the same way. There was no "learn and adapt" in their lexicon. The vast majority of the troopers Carrington brought to the Powder River Country had no experience in Indian warfare. Those who were veterans were well versed only in set pattern battles like those experienced in the Civil War. They applied those lessons (albeit out of context) which had resulted in success, to this new situation. It is another historical truth that conventional forces at the beginning will often try to use conventional tactics to defeat insurgents; and they most always fail.[73] With cooler weather and winter rapidly approached, the dwindling supply situation was getting serious. This caused Carrington to modify the post routine. It became obvious that his repeated requests for resupply were being ignored. At this point, Carrington's decision was to make preparations under the assumption they would have to last the winter without replenishment. Reinforcements arrived at Ft. Kearny in early November. The reinforcements consisted of forty-five infantrymen and one troop of sixty men from the

Second Cavalry. While any help was welcome, those green recruits arrived directly from the recruiting depot and could scarcely mount their horses without help.[74] Around the same time, young Capt Fetterman made his appearance along with several other replacement officers including Capt James Powell of the 2nd Cavalry. Powell was an interesting character. A steady, grizzled veteran with 13 years enlisted time under his belt, and he would soon become one of Carrington's most vocal critics.[75]

Shortly after the new officer's arrival, it became obvious that the discontent with Carrington's policies and strategies (or lack of) was gaining momentum. Carrington as a defensive thinker was a direct contradiction with that of the offensive minded replacement officers. Powell and Fetterman were both decorated Civil War heroes and their opinions held much weight with the men. However they found themselves bewildered by the hit-and-run guerilla tactics of the Indians whom refused to fight them toe to toe.[76] As fall turned to winter, the garrison at Ft Kearny, although secure behind the battlements of the stockade, was frustrated by the continued Sioux aggressions. They wanted to fight and show their mettle.[77] Never mind the fact that they were no more versed in Indian warfare than their commanding officer. What mattered to them was doing what soldiers do, and to "take the fight to the enemy." Shortly after his arrival and after consistent rejection from Carrington, Fetterman took matters into his own hands and began drilling his men in infantry tactics. Remember that these were the same men who had spent the last four months cooped up, while concentrating on construction of the fort. Most of these troops had entered Indian Wars service directly from the induction center in Missouri.[78]

At this point Carrington was in a vexing situation: his troop was spoiling for a fight, but the times when he did allow them to respond, they performed in erratic, unorthodox and often unauthorized pursuits.[79] It was ironic that after such success in the Civil War under like minded officers, Fetterman would be seconded to this remote outpost under a tactically opposite minded Carrington. Fetterman knew his commanding officer through reputation to be the consummate administrator, and of his comfortable wartime billet in the rear. Was General Cooke aware of this situation? Was he using it to test Carrington's leadership skills? One can only hope the CG did not use this combat campaign as a leadership laboratory, but he did allow it to happen. By late fall of 1866, Carrington was showing signs that he lacked in combat leadership skills. He had been observed at times to be, "inept, tolerant of insubordination, lenient towards offenders against discipline, hesitant when opposed, excitable under pressure, and defensive about his lack of command and combat experience."[80] Upon Fettermans arrival no doubt some "unofficial leadership" fell to him. The credibility he brought with him made him the natural leader for the rest of the junior officer corps. Indications were that his personal animosity and lack of respect for the commanding officer was sowing discord within the ranks. At one point Carrington tried to explain to his officers that the situation at hand required a defensive posture, and listed the reasons. But it fell on deaf ears. In fact, in a letter he wrote to a doctor friend giving his opinion on the matter, Fetterman replied, "give me 80 men and I can ride through the whole Indian nation!"[81] This was the statement he would become famous for. Fettermans' increasingly insubordinate behavior during the seven weeks he served at the fort indicated he was desperate to prove his superiority in battle against the Indians. This was a bad omen.[82]

In a surprising change of heart, once construction of the fort was complete in late November, Carrington indicated he would modify his strategy. In the first week of December he announced that the garrison would begin moving towards offensive operations. Previously, and displaying "an abysmal ignorance of the conditions in the Powder River," his boss General Cooke had issued explicit instructions for Carrington to go on the offensive and strike the Indians in their Winter camps.[83] This had been a commonly accepted Indian Wars strategy, to strike them when they had limited mobility. In turn, two weeks later Carrington promised his men, "to make the winter one of active operations in multiple different directions."[84] It quickly became evident that neglecting to train his soldiers for more than six months while constructing the fort was a mistake. This created a new tension among the officers, on one hand impatiently desiring to engage in battle knowing all the while that they were doing so with untrained troops. As was typical of the time, overconfidence and lack of respect for the enemy they faced overcame any apprehension in their minds.[85] Being well versed in what the "book" said, Carrington no doubt felt that a winter offensive took advantage of the one tactical benefit that seemed to favor him: that the Indians were less mobile in winter not just due to inclement weather, but also due to the scarcity of grass and game.[86] Therefore by mid December the small untrained garrison was switching gears from defense to offense. There was a growing dissension and discord within the ranks, and a commander feeling the pressure to "do something." It was a prelude to disaster.

The Lead Up To Battle

The events of December 21st and beyond were preceded by a series of small skirmishes. With the coming of cold weather, the Indian warriors initiated the tactic of attack and withdraw against the hay-cutting and woodcutting details. This resulted in small defensive breastworks at the pineries and large troop escorts for each detail.[87] The Indians knew they could never prevail in a head on assault upon the fort. However their numbers had grown to the point that they were confident they could destroy a contingent of any size provided they could trap them away from the fort. The Indian tacticians envisioned accomplishing this by feinted raids on the trains.[88]

On Dec 6 the wood train was attacked about an hour after leaving the fort. Upon receiving signals of the attack from Pilot Hill, Carrington dispatched Capt Fetterman, Lt Bingham and 30 cavalrymen to relieve the train and drive the Indians north. Carrington, Lt Grummond and 25 mounted infantrymen also rode out with the intention of circling around Lodge Trail Ridge and ambushing the retreating Indians in the Peno Valley. It would be a classic "hammer and anvil" tactic.[89] Everything went well at first; however, Carrington's anvil force was late getting into position. In pursuit of the fleeing enemy, Lt Bingham's cavalry got strung out, and shortly thereafter the Indians turned on them. In the melee Bingham galloped off after what surely was a decoy and was separated from his men. He was subsequently cutoff and shortly thereafter felled by arrows. Carrington in the meantime became involved in a running skirmish north of Lodge Trail Ridge, and successfully fought his way through the enemy with his saber. This was by far the largest engagement thus far for the garrison. While the Army escaped with little loss, the skirmish showed the brutal and bloody fighting common to the Indian Wars. It is noteworthy that even the cocky Capt Fetterman seemed sobered by the day's close quarters fighting. As he handed his official report to Carrington, he professed to have learned a lesson. He said, "This Indian war has become a hand-to-hand fight, requiring the utmost caution."[90]

In retrospect while this event was considered a tactical Army victory, it had an unintended consequence in affirming Sioux tactics, from which they drew clear conclusions. It convinced Red Cloud that a carefully crafted decoy tactic might work against a larger troop column, and that he possessed enough might to destroy any force Ft. Kearney might send to fight him. Since early that fall the Indians had been planning "two big fights with the whites, one at Pine Woods (Ft. Phil Kearney) and one at Big Horn (Ft. C.F. Smith)."[91] In the days following December 6, Red Cloud and the other chiefs came to an agreement. The time had come to combine their warriors in a great ambush, and lure the soldiers into the trap, employing their most able braves on their best ponies.[92] Two weeks later, the Indians made another probing attack using similar tactics.[93] This skirmish on December 19th again failed, but this time because Capt Powell refused to fall for the decoy trick and pursue them into a trap.[94] Ultimately, in the lead up to the Fetterman Battle, it was the Indians and not the Army that showed great ability to "learn and adapt" in their tactics. It seemed that with each raid they slightly modified the decoy tactic, and then tested it on the soldiers. And each time they adjusted just enough to add more friction to the fight, enhancing what Clausewitz called the "fog of war."[95] The Indians proved to be masters at conceiving creative ways to keep the soldiers guessing, and took advantage their relative inexperience. For the Indians in the lead up to the battle, the combination of good intelligence and a good battle strategy based on good Intel became a recipe for success. Conversely, a lack of Intelligence, or more precisely ignorance of obvious indicators combined with the predictability on army's part, resulted in just the opposite.

The Fetterman Massacre

On the morning of December 21st, 1866 at eleven o'clock, the Ft. Kearny wood train was attacked by Indians shortly after leaving the fort.[96] The wood train quickly circled to a defensive corral approximately one and a half miles from the post on the Sullivant Hills.[97] Col Carrington immediately ordered a rescue force assembled under the command of Capt Fetterman, consisting of forty-nine infantry. His orders from Carrington were, "support the wood train, relieve it, and report to me. Do not engage or pursue Indians at the wood train's expense; *under no circumstances pursue over Lodge Trail Ridge.*"[98] In interviews, witnesses unanimously agree that upon departure from the post, Fetterman did not proceed west along the Sullivant Hills toward the wood train.[99] Rather, he was observed moving northeast directly toward Lodge Trail Ridge in what must be interpreted as an attempt to cutoff the retreating Indian raiders.[100] As the column made its way across the valley, Carrington was watching the progress from the lookout tower atop the headquarters building.[101] We shall assume that Fetterman departed the fort with every intention to obey the orders of his commanding officer.

If Carrington observed the infantry proceeding into trouble and disobeying his orders, he had more than enough time to have easily recalled the column. In fact, shortly after the soldiers departed the fort, the Indians broke off the attack on the wood train and retreated toward Lodge Trail Ridge. Those retreating Indians included the famed Sioux warrior Crazy Horse. They subsequently withdrew to the top of Lodge Trail Ridge, and from there they proceeded to taunt the soldiers, in an attempt to lure them into Peno Valley. With the wood train no longer under attack, according to orders Fetterman's infantry column should have returned to the post. But they didn't, and no one made any attempt to stop them. The fact that Carrington allowed the slowly

31

progressing column to continue directly at, up and eventually over Lodge Trail Ridge suggests that this could have been an offensive strategy which was previously agreed upon. The initial actions of the day suggest that this was a planned offensive, and if successful would have been a major coup for all involved. Many historians may still place partial blame on Fetterman for ignoring direct orders, but the record indicates that may not be true. At any rate, shortly after departure Carrington directed Lt Grummond and twenty-seven mounted cavalrymen armed with seven shot repeating Spencer carbines, along with two civilians armed with repeating Henry rifles to join Fetterman's column. Carrington's orders were, "report to brevet Lieutenant Colonel Fetterman, implicitly obey orders, *and do not leave him.*"[102] As they thundered out the gate, they were observed riding straight off in the direction of Fetterman's column. In the meantime, Fetterman's infantry column seemed to accelerate as if in a rush to contact. And instead of paralleling the Sullivant Hills which would have been a line to the wood train, the relief column continued marching directly toward Lodge Trail Ridge.

Lt Grummond had previously shown a propensity for getting his cavalry perilously strung out. In a previous skirmish he exhibited the tendency to rush to contact and chase raiders into a trap, and it nearly cost him his life. On this day, his orders were to ride and join the infantry column, thereby protecting Fetterman's flank which was standard operating procedure of the era. He was expressly forbidden to venture ahead of it unless so directed by Fetterman. Lt Grummond and the cavalry were observed quickly overtaking, then joining the infantry column in its normally assigned position. But shortly thereafter, they pushed ahead in front of the column on a line up and over Lodge Trail Ridge in pursuit of the Indians. What awaited the troopers in was an ambush force of unprecedented size: more than two thousand Sioux, Cheyenne and Arapahoe warriors.[103] Red Cloud's choice of the Peno Valley on the reverse slope of Lodge Trail Ridge and nestled in rolling terrain allowed the massive ambushing force to remain in defilade, hidden until the trap was sprung. Another key advantage was that the ambush force behind the hills is kept in defilade from the cannon at the fort. The Indian plan of attack was superb: they used decoy tactics masterfully; they adroitly hid an overwhelming force using terrain and concealment to their advantage; and they applied previously gained tendencies and Intel gathered on the troops and lured them into a devastating ambush.

Once Grummond's cavalry was out ahead of the main column, his men were separated, and cutoff from the infantry. Fetterman may have felt he had no choice but to follow in an attempt to save his fellow troops-even against direct orders. Carrington's orders were designed to mitigate Indian decoy tactics by not chasing the raiders and thus avoiding ambushes unless of course pursuit was the plan all along. As Carrington watched the entire force disappear over the ridge, what he couldn't see beyond in Peno Valley would equal his worst nightmare. At approximately noon, the Indians sprang the ambush.[104] Grummond managed to halt his cavalry and Fetterman's infantry quickly closed the gap. Under a deluge of arrows and with the experienced Civil War veterans in the lead, the troopers dismounted and quickly took defensive positions.[105] At some point as the battle progressed, Fetterman may have attempted a retrograde back up the hill and there formed another defensive position in close proximity to a rock formation for cover.[106] Eventually Lt Grummond and his sergeant became separated from the other two positions and were killed. How the battle progressed and the order of death can only be reconstructed from the positions found, locations of expended brass and later Indian accounts. Prophetically, the exact number of troops with which Fetterman boasted he could run through the whole Indian nation was in fact the number of troopers killed this day. All eighty-one trapped men were killed in this as yet unprecedented massacre of the Indian Wars. The different positions were overrun starting with Fetterman's line.

At some point Fetterman was joined by cavalry Lt Brown. It has been commonly held that Fetterman and Brown saved their last bullets and committed mutual suicide rather than be caught and tortured, but new evidence says something quite different. Army surgeon autopsy reports and Indian accounts of the battle say that Fetterman was knocked down by American Horse with a 3 foot long war club. Then the warrior dismounted and slit his throat in a "coup de gras."[107] Close on the heels of the infantry position being overrun, the initial defensive position was as well. Indications found at the scene showed a desperate ending with civilians Wheatley and Fisher along with six infantryman battling hand to hand using gunstocks, bayonets and knives until the last man expired.[108] At that point in the battle, those still surviving were strung out along the hill in pockets of men desperately fighting for their lives. As Indian lookouts signaled that a relief column was approaching, the commanding chiefs sent word to kill the remaining soldiers as quickly as possible.[109] This final thrust by the Indians was against small pockets of soldiers holding out amongst the boulders. The soldiers in these positions fought gallantly until they were out of ammunition and overrun. Giving indication of the ferocity of the final moments of battle, the majority of the Indian casualties occurred in the final push. One of the last to soldiers to die, the veteran Army bugler Adolph Metzger, evidently fought off the last of his attackers with his bent and twisted bugle until finally succumbing to over a dozen wounds.[110]

Prior to withdrawing from the battlefield, the Indians stripped and mutilated the bodies of the soldiers according to cultural beliefs.[111] It is noteworthy that the only body left unmutilated was that of bugler Metzger. His body was found covered by a buffalo robe as the Indian ultimate sign of respect for bravery in battle.[112] The battle from start to finish had taken approximately forty minutes.[113] In that time, over forty thousand arrows had been expended- a thousand a minute by an estimated two thousand Indians armed with a combination of the bow, rifles, lances and war clubs.[114] With no U.S. soldier survivors to interview, the estimated number of Indian casualties is based on evidence from the battlefield later observed by the relief column. However, later Indian interviews indicate a reliable estimate of Indian warriors killed at between 50 and 200.[115]

Shortly after shots were heard coming from the direction of Peno Creek; Capt Tendor Ten Eyck was dispatched along with the remaining infantry, cavalry and two wagons.[116] His orders were to join Fetterman at all hazards. However, within thirty minutes of departure and just as the relief party was cresting Lodge Trail Ridge; the battle came to an end. Ten Eyck observed groups of Indians below and in the surrounding valleys for miles, committing depredations and taunting the soldiers to come down and fight. He wisely chose not to succumb to emotion and fall for the same ruse which got so many of his fellow soldiers killed that day. As the Indians began to disperse, the relief column moved cautiously forward with the wagons. They finally reached the field of battle where they recovered forty-nine bodies-including those of Fetterman and Brown.[117] Due to approaching darkness, and a large enemy force nearby, they suspended their efforts for the night and recovered to the fort. Ten Eyck was forever criticized for taking a less than direct route to the scene of the fighting. Many said that had he had gone directly to the sounds of the battle he may have saved some lives.

Upon returning to the fort, there was a sense that the garrison was under siege and in serious trouble. There were only 119 men left to defend the women and children in the fort against the thousands of Indian warriors known to be nearby. The garrison spent a long, anxious night expecting another attack at any moment-but that never came. After surviving the night, the job the next morning was to recover the rest of the bodies. While venturing outside the fort and going back to the battlefield would be hazardous, they knew the bodies had to be recovered at all costs.[118] Carrington himself led the recovery force of eighty men. The scene was a gruesome one. There were frozen bodies strewn throughout the valley in various states of mutilation. Here Carrington goes into great detail elaborating the desecration in his official report.[119] In it he notes scenes of obvious extreme valor and bravery against tremendous odds. He notes the defensive position of the two civilians Wheatley and Fisher, and how there were heaps of expended brass and many blood stained spots surrounding their position. It was a testament to the ferocity with which they fought. He noted that one of them was found with "one hundred and five arrows in his naked body."[120] He also goes on to explain why the Indians performed depredations and mutilations on fallen enemy at the battlefield" by mutilating the bodies: removing eyes, eviscerating, cutting off heads and limbs, etc., the Indians are preventing the enemy the ability to enjoy the trappings of paradise and the happy hunting grounds of the afterlife.[121]

As darkness approached and snow began to fall, Carrington recovered his men and the rest of the bodies back to Ft. Kearny. The weather continued to worsen as the night progressed into near blizzard conditions. With his total force reduced by one third Carrington prepared the fort for an expected follow on Indian attack sometime over the next few days. Because the garrison included women and children, and knowing what the Indians would do to the innocents if they were captured, a drastic last ditch measure was prepared. A fortified defense bunker was built on top of the powder magazine where the women and children would be placed should the stockade be in peril. In the magazine he rigged a tremendous charge which would be ignited if all was lost, to prevent capture by the Indians.

About the same time Carrington penned a message reporting the attack, to be taken via courier to Horseshow Station on the Platte River for transmittal to Omaha, and then onto Ft. Laramie. Civilian worker John "Portuguese" Phillips volunteered to ride as courier and then departed on his classic four day/236 mile ride thru hostile Indian territory in howling blizzard conditions. After 190 miles he reached Horseshoe Station to send the message via telegraph and where he dropped off companion riders. Phillips then continued on alone, arriving late on a snowy, frigid Christmas night. The appearance of the huge form of Phillips, dressed in his ice encrusted buffalo overcoat, pants, gauntlet and cap at the Christmas dress ball immediately brought a hush to the crowd. His arrival at Laramie must have made a shocking scene, appearing like an apparition out of the maelstrom. The message of the attack immediately generated frantic preparation for a rescue column. However, the departure was delayed by deep snows until 6 January. Those two weeks were a tense period of waiting for those at the Ft Kearney garrison.[122]

In January, Lt Colonel Henry W. Wessells arrived from Ft Reno with a relief column. He had previously been selected as post commander to free Carrington to pursue his Mountain District command duties. With him he brought additional troops from Ft. Laramie and supplies. This change of command had been planned for some time, and was part of the Army reorganization and not directly related to the massacre though many at the time felt it was. For the first time since the battalion arrived back in July, it was fully garrisoned with troops and equipment. Ironically, it took a massacre to get headquarters to finally send the items Carrington had been requesting from the beginning. The Mountain District headquarters was being moved to Ft. Casper, and on January 25th Carrington took sixty soldiers as escort along with the women and children, and proceeded to Casper again in the midst of a driving snowstorm. During the journey, the frigid conditions caused many lost fingers and toes from frostbite.

In postscript, the War and Indian Affairs Departments were quick to find a scapegoat for the tragedy. General Cooke placed overall blame squarely on the shoulders of the commanding officer. Interestingly, the Dept of Indian Affairs reason given for the Indians attack was that they were "rendered desperate due to starvation."[123] The public opinion was equally damning and Carrington received the blame in the national press, while at the same time Fetterman was lauded as a "national hero." Carrington would eventually retire four years after the Fetterman fight. Ultimately even General Cooke did not escape blame, and was replaced on January 9th, 1867 as commander of the Department of the Platte by Gen Grant

After Effects of the Battle

The Army of 1866 knew nothing of information operations. The limited ability to communicate from western posts radically affected public opinion. It allowed the press to use their imagination and fill in the gaps, jumping to conclusions before getting all the facts. It was a bad thing for the military then and it still isn't today. Filling in those gaps helped to reinforce in the public mind that Carrington must have been to blame. And for the same reason, Fetterman was treated as both a hero and a martyr for the Indian Wars. In the case of the Fetterman massacre, it would be many years until the official report would finally be released. Carrington claimed that his own accounts of what happened were censured, or at the least unreasonably delayed. He did spend the rest of his life, along with his second wife, working hard to clear his name. As late as the summer of 1908, Carrington was the keynote speaker for the Fourth of July celebration, marking the "Fortieth Anniversary of the Opening of Wyoming" and a reunion of Ft Phil Kearny survivors in Sheridan, Wyoming.[124] In his lengthy monologue he continued to assert his innocence. He emphasized his valiant performances and the many wrongs done to him by history.[125] For many years, wife Frances Carrington blamed Fetterman and defended her husband in books, writings and speaking engagements. Unfortunately for Fetterman, he left no family behind to defend his name. Instead, his record was affirmed via the testimony of the officers and soldiers who worked with him, when given during inquiries into the battle that bears his name.[126] On February 18th, 1867 President Andrew Johnson appointed a joint commission of military officers and civilians to investigate the Fetterman Massacre, and determine steps necessary to prevent it from happening again.[127] The Sanborn Commission as it came to be known took over six months to investigate the matter fully. Upon completion its results were clouded by controversy, and there were signs of politically motivated meddling.[128] While

Carrington fared better in this case, as the report confirmed that he several times

repeated the order "not to pursue" over Lodge Trail Ridge, it still included damaging

testimony that remained questionable in origin. It ultimately concluded that the

Department of the Platte did not provide the Bozeman Trail forts with enough troops or

supplies for peacetime-let alone enough for war! Unfortunately the government buried

the report in Indian Bureau files where it was to languish until the early 20th Century.[129]

The final report eventually cleared and exonerated Carrington, but he never really shed

the stigma of being in command during the second worst U.S. Army defeat of the Indian

Wars. Carrington's case was not bolstered by later devastating testimony from Capt

James Powell (whom himself became a national hero at the Wagon Box fight), who

confirmed his commander's fault and negligence. Not till much later would Carrington's

name be exonerated in the tragic affair.

From the government there seemed to be a laissez-faire attitude regarding the

Powder River Country in 1866. Not only did General Cooke seem unconcerned, but

General Sherman had urged the officers to take their wives with them, obviously

viewing any problem in the Powder River Country as insignificant.[130] Interestingly just

days before the Fetterman fight, President Andrew Johnson publicly declared that the

Army was well armed and well supported and that the Plains Indians "have

unconditionally submitted to our authority and manifested an earnest desire for a

renewal of friendly relations." And he was clearly unaware of the public statements

made by Red Cloud at Ft. Laramie. Sometime after the events of 1866, General of the

Army Ulysses S. Grant would be the master of understatement in a letter to Secretary of

War Stanton (which was later published in western newspapers), that "(a) standing army could not prevent occasional Indian outrages, no matter what its magnitude."[131]

In this event, there were examples of failure in command at multiple levels. In his reports to headquarters, Carrington repeatedly emphasized the urgent situation to his direct superior, General Phillip Cooke. Records indicate that Cooke did approve the requisitions, but never had the sense of urgency to follow through ensuring they were drawn, shipped and delivered.[132] While logistical problems were a fact of life in the 1866 Army of the West, including the lack of telegraph and railroad in many parts that seriously hampered operations; as commanding general of the Dept of the Platte, Cooke was directly responsible to ensure he sent the proper numbers of trained and equipped troops, at which the record has shown he failed.[133]

In July 1867, Indian forces led by Red Cloud and Crazy Horse attempted to repeat their earlier victory by again attacking woodcutters and soldiers, this time camped about five miles from Fort C.F. Smith in what was to be known as the Wagon Box Fight. This was to be the second large attack envisioned and planned by Red Cloud to force the white soldiers to abandon the Bozeman Trail. In this case, an estimated one to two thousand Indians sprang the attack against twenty-six soldiers and six civilians under the command of Capt. James Powell. The defenders took cover behind a series of wagon boxes arrayed in an oval which had been used as a stock corral. Powell's men managed to hold off the much larger force until a relief column from the fort arrived.[134]

By August 1867, the Army had modified about 50,000 Civil War surplus Springfield rifles to fire metal cartridges from the breech. This was known as the Allin

41

Conversion.[135] The effect on the Sioux at Wagon Box was noticeable surprise. The rate

of fire of the modified weapons repulsed them repeatedly both at the Wagon Box and

Hayfield fights. The defeats can be directly attributed can be directly attributed to the

Allin converted Springfield rifles recently issued to the Twenty Seventh Infantry.[136] This

had a telling psychological effect on the Indians. The attackers possessed more than

enough warriors to overrun troops but weren't able to; and the defenders incorporated

at least some lessons learned from the Fetterman fight quite successfully. Powell would

become a national hero at a time when the nation sorely needed one.[137] The

significance of the Wagon Box Fight to the Army was that it reinforced a long

established tenet that a small, well armed defensive force established in a strong

position will enjoy a tactical advantage over a numerically superior foe. In fact this

scenario would be repeated a number of times later on in subsequent battles.[138] Right

on the heels of the Wagon Box Fight, a battle occurred on August 1st, three miles from

Ft. C.F. Smith this time pitting thirty-one soldiers & civilians against more than 700

Sioux and Cheyenne warriors. As the Hayfield Fight battle commenced, the men

hunkered down behind a low log corral barrier and proceeded to hold off the Indians for

more than six hours. They were finally relieved by a column sent from the fort, which

duly disbursed the Indians[139]

In both of these fights the Indians lost the battle but accomplished their strategic

goals, and in early 1867 the U.S. government determined that the Bozeman Trail could

not be secured and closed it to travel forever.[140] It was a law of diminishing returns that

the troops stationed along the trail had their hands full just defending themselves, let

alone protecting travel along the trail. By August of 1868 the troops had abandoned both Ft. Phil Kearney and C.F. Smith and moved back down the trail to Ft. Reno. Sometime after their departure, the Indians burnt both forts to the ground, in essence ridding themselves of the "last vestiges white man" in their sacred hunting grounds. The Lakota, Cheyenne and Arapahoe nations had successfully halted civilian travel into their land. They had decisively defended those lands from the Army through aggressive insurgent tactics. After the troops cleared out of the country, Red Cloud finally signed a peace treaty at Ft. Laramie on 6 Nov 1868. At that time, the U.S. government conceded that the Powder River Country was near "sovereign Indian Territory," and that the whites needed their consent to pass through it.

To the Indians, the Fetterman victory—known to Sioux as "Battle of 100 Slain," became the stuff of legend which would be passed by word of mouth to descendants for many years to come.[141] For Chief Red Cloud, this was his swan song as an Indian warrior and leader. He would never take to the war path again.

Following the events of 1866 and the closure of the Bozeman Trail, the U.S. Army and the nation shifted its focus but never really changed its Fabian strategy. The emphasis on winning by wearing down Indian resistance through numerous small permanent garrisons throughout the west was not working.[142] It was not until late 1876 that manpower on the northern plains would be sufficient to decisively defeat the Lakotas, and shift to a more offensive strategic campaign.[143] In July 1867, J.B. Weston, who had wintered at Ft. Phil Kearney in 1866, testified before the Sanborn Committee investigating the Fetterman Massacre. He summarized the Army's misguided strategy, saying "The War Department has failed to appreciate its extent and magnitude (Red Clouds War)," and that the Army "has sent a military force into this country so small, inadequate, and insufficient in numbers, arms and supplies, that instead of conquering a peace, it has aggravated and augmented the troubles."[144] Unfortunately, for many reasons—many of same mistakes would be repeated tragically ten years later at Little Bighorn.

Afghan War Similarities

There are many parallels between the Indian Wars of the 19th Century, and the Afghanistan Campaign in the 21st Century. There have been different "ages" of insurgency for the United States: the Indian Wars stretched from the 17th Century to the end of the 19th Century, then there were the insurgencies like that which occurred in the Philippines of the early 20th Century, followed by the more modern type insurgencies like the Vietnam War. Each era differed from the others in some ways, and required counterinsurgency forces to adapt to the changes. The same type of adaptation has applied in Afghanistan.[145] Many times, however, the Army found itself not adapting to change, but relearning lessons it had forgotten from previous campaigns. Once it became clear that the U.S. Army would be fighting in Afghanistan over the long term, people started referring to the enemy and fighting there as "new" type of fighting; but in fact it was not new. History has shown that while similarities abound between the Indian Wars and the Afghan campaign, there are also significant differences. It is important in historical case studies to show both sides. But in this case, the similarities are significant enough to note in a historical context, clearly showing that the U.S. has been in conflicts like that in Afghanistan before.

In both the Indian Wars and Afghanistan, the United States has been far superior in numbers, technology, and wealth. The enemy in each case was cunning and ruthless, and seemed to adroitly counter our main advantages in a manner that suited their strengths. The enemy in both cases was a tribal based society with a warrior ethos that put a premium on fighting ability. These cultures liked to fight: whether against tribal competitors or when appropriate united against a common invading foe. It cannot be assumed that as in most civilized societies, the populace even desires a peaceful solution. When war is all that is known, it becomes the norm. If it is a culture's nature to be warlike, then it is extremely difficult to change. The United States government took a similar approach in each case by attempting to apply western models of governance, when in reality those models would never work. These tribal societies were primitive, and existed for hundreds, if not thousands, of years without a semblance of an organized governing body. The American Indians governed within tribes based on seniority and fighting prowess. The Afghan tribes operated in a similar manner with tribal elders, village headmen, or sometimes regional warlords dictating law. In neither case was a central government able to reign supreme. The Indians were eventually subdued, relegated to designated reservations, and "Americanized." There will be no such "Americanization" in Afghanistan. It remains to be seen then whether the American model will take hold in Afghanistan where such huge differences in culture and ideology exist. In fact, the road to that point may ultimately prove to be unnavigable. Such deeply engrained cultural norms cannot be changed over the short term, but will require a long term approach.

Tactically, similarities abound between the two conflicts. The tactics used by the Indians were very similar to those used by the Taliban. The Indians were creative in prosecuting a hybrid type of insurgent warfare that mitigated the Army's overwhelming strength by developing a highly successful decoy strategy. Similarly, the Taliban rarely engage Army forces head on, but instead rely on deception with ambush tactics. Both the Taliban and the Indians showed the ability to mix, hide, and melt into the civilian populace at their convenience. Such tactics pose a dilemma in distinguishing friend from foe, and can inject doubt into the minds of soldiers or even force unduly restrictive rules of engagement.

In each situation, the combatants were locked in a fight to defend their survival interests. With the Sioux, that included Army troops trespassing upon their sacred hunting grounds, mass extermination of the buffalo and ultimately the cessation of their way of life. The Taliban survival interests include the establishment of the caliphate, Sharia Law and the declared Muslim holy war. When a society sees an enemy as a direct threat to their survival, they become willing to expend any means to accomplish their goals and prevent extinction.

Technology has been a key advantage for the United States in both eras. Such an overwhelming superiority in technology and firepower was mitigated somewhat by the enemy in both campaigns, through the ingenious use of crude, but effective weapons. The Indians used bows, arrows and war clubs, and tended to dictate the time and place of their engagements to maximize their effectiveness. Exemplified in the Fetterman Battle, the Indians applied their decoy tactic and used advantageous terrain to minimize the effectiveness of the Army's technologically superior weapons. In Afghanistan, the Taliban performed similarly. They rarely engage the Army directly, but rely on ambush similarly using time and terrain to their benefit. They have adopted the use of IEDs, indirect fire using rockets, and small arms applied in situations designed to maximize their impact. In both the Indian Wars and Afghanistan, the insurgents possessed a strong and charismatic leader: Chief Red Cloud for the Lakota Sioux and Osama Bin Laden for the radical Muslims.

The theater and context in which each campaign took place holds similarities as well. In each theater of battle, the people possessed a natural xenophobia, distrust and dislike of outsiders.[146] With the Indians, this was countered in a variety of ways including bribery through food and gifts, trickery through the use of treaties, and sheer force. In Afghanistan this presents a paradigm to overcome in employing COIN doctrine. Such overwhelmingly distrustful populations there make it unlikely the U.S. and its allies will ever win the "hearts and minds." The current strategy, which applies power across the spectrum of the DIME, may in fact be one way to overcome this disadvantage.

Each of the campaigns possessed similarly daunting logistical dilemmas. For the U.S. Army, while possessing numerical superiority and overwhelming advantages in equipment and supply, each required extremely long lines of supply. This ultimately became a major center of gravity which the enemy attacked repeatedly. The terrain in each theater is rugged and mountainous, prone to harsh weather, and required austere remote forts and outposts to be manned against a cunning, mobile, and elusive enemy whose tactics differ greatly from the U.S. Army. Ft. Phil Kearny was at the very end of the line deep in Indian Country. Similarly today, outpost Restropo represents the Army's most extreme remote garrison in Afghanistan.

There were clear similarities then, between the U.S. Army's Indian Wars Campaign and the Afghanistan Campaign. Much can be learned from both the Army's successes and the mistakes in the Indian Wars, and can be applied to the current insurgency in Afghanistan. While the context of the time period plays a role in determining relevancy, there are lessons to be learned from old insurgent conflicts which can apply to the modern battlefield.

Conclusions

Nearly 150 years have passed since the events of Red Cloud's War and the Fetterman Massacre. Yet the lessons learned from the Indian Wars are still appropriate for our troops waging battle against insurgents in Afghanistan. The downsizing post Civil War Army of 1866 found itself with competing agendas: Secure a reconstructing south, defend the transcontinental railroad, and fight an ever growing insurgency against American Indians in the Great Plains and across the west. Against an uprising in the Powder River Country they sent a force much too small and under equipped to defend and protect immigrants along the Bozeman Trail. Caught in this impossible task were officers with conflicting personalities and styles. Failure to adequately equip and train the soldiers, ignorance of obvious indicators and intelligence of coming trouble, and ultimately a lack of leadership at many levels culminated in the worst single defeat for the U.S. Army up to that point: the Fetterman Massacre. In its aftermath came blame and reluctance to accept responsibility. Ultimately the U.S. government decided to close the Bozeman Trail forever. Through an aggressive insurgent strategy, the Indians had won the day. The U.S. would see similar scenarios throughout the 20th Century and beyond. In this case, not until nearly ten years later would the U.S. Army figure out a strategy to successfully combat the Indian insurgency, in no short measure aided by the opening of the transcontinental railroad in 1869.

As we've seen, the Powder River Campaign was the first U.S. Army war against an irregular insurgent force. With that come many similarities to the current battle against insurgency in Afghanistan. In both, the long supply line made it a critically important and possibly the key center of gravity for the enemy to exploit. As the cliché goes, "the past holds the key to the future." Technology has changed tactics over the years, but a strategy which accounts for human nature may remain the same over the millennia. When it comes down to it, humans will fight to defend their survival interests. It's not a stretch when looking at an early photo of military officers sitting in a circle with Indians having council or "pow-wow" over some grievance; just as we have seen young officers doing in Afghanistan with the local tribal elders. The times, places, names and combatants are different, but the human nature of the conduct of insurgent war remains the same. Clearly then, Red Cloud's War and the Indian Wars in general can provide us with many lessons learned to help in the fight against insurgents of the 21st Century. Military history and the study of past insurgencies have always been important to military leaders. The lessons we gain through the study of history matter more today than ever.

Endnotes

[1] Sebastian L.v. Gorka and Davis Kilcullen, "An Actor-centric Theory of War," *Joint Force Quarterly* 60, (1st Quarter 2011): 15.

[2] Ibid.

[3] R. Eli Paul, ed., *Autobiography of Red Cloud* (Helena, MT: Montana Historical Society Press, 1997), 189.

[4] General Henry B. Carrington, *The Indian Question* (New York: Sol Lewis, 1973), i.

[5] Carl von Clausewitz, *On War*, Michael Howard and Peter Paret, eds. And trans. (Princeton, N.J.: Princeton Univ. Press, 1976), p.75.

[6] Ibid., 87.

[7] Cyrus Townsend Brady, *Indian Fights and Fighters* (General Books, 2009), 5-6.

[8] B.F. McCune and Louis Hart, "The Fatal Fetterman Fight," December 1997, http://www.historynet.com/the-fatal-fetterman-fight.htm (accessed December 20, 2010).

[9] John H. Monnett, *Where a Hundred Soldiers Were Killed* (Albuquerque: University of New Mexico Press, 2008), 77.

[10] U.S. Joint Chiefs of Staff, *Department of Defense Dictionary of Military and Associated Terms*, Joint Publication 1-02 (Washington, DC: U.S. Joint Chiefs of Staff, June 13, 2007), 265

[11] U.S. Department of the Army, *Counterinsurgency*, Army Field Manual 3-24 (Washington, DC: U.S. Department of the Army, December 2006), 1-1.

[12] U.S. Department of the Army, *The United States Army Operating Concept*, TRADOC Pamphlet 525-3-1 (Washington, DC: U.S. Department of the Army, August 19, 2010), 26.

[13] U.S. Department of the Army, *Counterinsurgency*, ix.

[14] H Ripley Rawlings IV, "Effects Based Operations: Defined Through the Mistakes of the Past," *Armor* 114, no.6 (November/December 2005): 31, in ProQuest (accessed December 1, 2010).

[15] Robert M. Utley, *Frontiersmen in Blue* (New York: The Macmillan Company, 1967), 330-331.

[16] Robert M. Utley, *Frontier Regulars* (New York: Macmillan Publishing Co., Inc., 1973), 14.

[17] Ibid., 15.

[18] Ibid.

[19] Brady, *Indian Fights and Fighters*, 6.

[20] Jerry Keenan, *The Wagon Box Fight* (Conshohocken, PA: Savas Publishing Company, 2000), 37

[21] Michael Clodfelter, *The Dakota War* (Jefferson, NC: McFarland & Company, Inc., Publishers, 1998), 14.

[22] Ibid.

[23] Ibid., 11.

[24] Ibid.

[25] Ibid., 12.

[26] U.S. Department of the Army, *Counterinsurgency*, 1-11.

[27] Utley, *Frontier Regulars*, 46

[28] Ibid., 47.

[29] Ibid.

[30] Ibid., 53.

[31] Ibid., 48.

[32] Meredith Hindley, "Where Settlers and Sioux Collided: A Bozeman Retrospective," *Humanities* 20, no.4 (July/August 1999): 28, in ProQuest (accessed December 1, 2010).

[33] Monnett, *Where a Hundred Soldiers Were Killed*, 64.

[34] Brady, *Indian Fights and Fighters*, 7.

[35] Utley, *Frontier Regulars*, 103.

[36] Brady, *Indian Fights and Fighters*, 8.

[37] Rawlings, "Effects-based Operations," 28

[38] Ibid., 29.

[39] Monnett, *Where a Hundred Soldiers Were Killed*, 23.

[40] Ibid.

[41] Ibid.

[42] Rawlings, "Effects-based Operations," 29.

[43] Paul, *Autobiography of Red Cloud*, 189.

[44] Margaret Irvin Carrington, *Ab-Sa-Ra-Ka* (Philadelphia: J.B. Lippincott & Co., 1868), 73.

[45] McCune and Hart, "The Fatal Fetterman Fight," 2.

[46] Carrington, *Ab-Sa-Ra-Ka*, 74.

[47] Utley, *Frontier Regulars*, 103-104.

[48] Ibid., 51.

[49] McCune and Hart, "The Fatal Fetterman Fight," 2.

[50] Carrington, *Ab-Sa-Ra-Ka*, 93.

[51] Utley, *Frontier Regulars*, 104.

[52] Carrington, *Ab-Sa-Ra-Ka*, 94-95.

[53] U.S. Department of the Army, *Counterinsurgency*, 3-2.

[54] Utley, *Frontier Regulars*, 54.

[55] Ibid.

[56] McCune and Hart, "The Fatal Fetterman Fight," 2.

[57] Ibid.

[58] Brady, *Indian Fights and Fighters*, 11-12.

[59] "Fort Phil Kearny, Dakota Territory, 1866-1868," http://www.philkearny.vcn.com/ fortphilkearny.htm (accessed December 20, 2010).

[60] Brady, *Indian Fights and Fighters*, 12.

[61] Col. Henry B. Carrington, "History of Indian Operations on the plains, furnished to a special commission which met at Fort McPherson, Nebr., in the Spring of 1867." 14.

[62] McCune and Hart, "The Fatal Fetterman Fight," 2.

[63] Carrington, *Ab-Sa-Ra-Ka*, 123-129.

[64] Ibid., 129.

[65] Utley, *Frontier Regulars*, 104.

[66] Carrington, "Indian Operations on the Plains," 14.

[67] Ibid.

[68] Ibid., 71.

[69] Henry B. Carrington, *The Indian Question: Including a Report by the Secretary of the Interior on the Massacre of Troops Near Fort Kearny, December 1866* (Boston, 1884), 21.

[70] U.S. Department of the Army, *Counterinsurgency*, ix.

[71] Utley, *Frontier Regulars*, 14.

[72] Monnett, *Where a Hundred Soldiers Were Killed*, 76.

[73] U.S. Department of the Army, *Counterinsurgency*, ix.

[74] Utley, *FrontierRegulars*, 107.

[75] Ibid.

[76] Monnett, *Where a Hundred Soldiers Were Killed*, 52.

[77] Ibid.

[78] Shannon Smith Calitri, "Give Me Eighty Men," *Montana; the Magazine of Western History*, Autumn 2004, 48.

[79] Utley, *Frontier Regulars*, 104.

[80] Ibid., 103.

[81] McCune and Hart, "The Fatal Fetterman Fight," 3.

[82] Caltri, "Give Me Eighty Men," 46.

[83] Utley, *Frontier Regulars*, 107.

[84] Ibid.

[85] Ibid., 106.

[86] Ibid., 54.

[87] Monnett, *Where a Hundred Soldiers Were Killed*, 53.

[88] Ibid.

[89] McCune and Hart, "The Fatal Fetterman Fight," 3.

[90] Dee Brown, *The Fetterman Massacre* (Lincoln, NE: University of Nebraska Press, 1962), 166.

[91] Utley, *Frontier Regulars*, 108.

[92] Brown, *The Fetterman Massacre*, 172.

[93] Ibid., 173.

[94] Utley, *Frontier Regulars*, 108.

[95] Clausewitz, *On War*, 101.

[96] Carrington, *The Indian Question*, 22.

[97] Ibid.

[98] Ibid.

[99] Calitri, "Give Me Eighty Men," 48.

[100] Ibid.

[101] Ibid.

[102] Carrington, *The Indian Question*, 22.

[103] Brown, *The Fetterman Massacre*, 178.

[104] Carrington, *The Indian Question*, 23.

[105] Brown, *The Fetterman Massacre*, 179.

[106] Ibid., 180.

[107] McCune and Hart, "The Fatal Fetterman Fight," 5.

[108] Brown, *The Fetterman Massacre*, 181.

[109] Ibid., 182.

[110] Ibid.

[111] Ibid., 183.

[112] Ibid.

[113] Carrington, *The Indian Question*, 23.

[114] Brown, *The Fetterman Massacre*, 183.

[115] Ibid.

[116] Carrington, *The Indian Question*, 23.

[117] Ibid.

[118] Ibid.

[119] Ibid., 25.

[120] Ibid., 24.

[121] Ibid., 9.

[122] "The Famous Ride of John "Portuguese" Phillips," http://www.philkearny.vcn.com/ phillips.htm (accessed December 20, 2010).

[123] McCune and Hart, "The Fatal Fetterman Fight," 7.

[124] Calitri, "Give Me Eighty Men," 55.

[125] Ibid., 57.

[126] Calitri, "Give Me Eighty Men," 51.

[127] Shannon D. Smith, *Give Me Eighty Men: Women and the Myth of the Fetterman Fight* (Lincoln, NE: University of Nebraska Press, 2008), 147.

[128] Ibid., 147-158.

[129] Monnett, *Where a Hundred Soldiers Were Killed*, xxxii.

[130] Ibid, 91.

[131] Ibid.

[132] Calitri, "Give Me Eighty Men," 51.

[133] Ibid., 50.

[134] "The Wagon Box Fight," http://www.philkearny.vcn.com/wagonboxfight.htm (accessed December 20, 2010).

[135] Utley, *Frontier Regulars*, 71-72.

[136] Ibid., 73.

[137] Calitri, "Give Me Eighty Men,"

[138] Keenan, *The Wagon Box Fight*, 46.

[139] "Hayfield Fight (1867)," linked from *Legends of America Home Page* at ""Battles and Massacres of the Indian Wars in the American West," http://www.legendsofamerica.com/na-indianwarbattles-2.html (accessed December 19, 2010.

[140] Monnett, *Where a Hundred Soldiers Were Killed*, 71.

[141] McCune and Hart, "The Fatal Fetterman Fight," 7.

[142] Monnett, *Where a Hundred Soldiers Were Killed*, 71.

[143] Ibid., 237.

[144] Ibid., 92.

[145] Steven Metz and Raymond Millen, "Insurgency in Iraq and Afghanistan: Change And Continuity," *Strategic Studies Institute*, 2.

[146] Ibid., 14.